Idaho

Jim Ollhoff

Visit us at
www.abdopublishing.com

Published by ABDO Publishing Company, 8000 West 78th Street, Suite 310, Edina, Minnesota 55439 USA. Copyright ©2010 by Abdo Consulting Group, Inc. International copyrights reserved in all countries. No part of this book may be reproduced in any form without written permission from the publisher. The Checkerboard Library™ is a trademark and logo of ABDO Publishing Company.

Printed in the United States.

Editor: John Hamilton
Graphic Design: Sue Hamilton
Cover Illustration: Neil Klinepier
Cover Photo: iStock Photo
Interior Photo Credits: Alamy, AP Images, Boise Hawks, Comstock, Corbis, Getty, Granger Collection, Idaho Falls Chukars, Idaho Stampede, Idaho Steelheads, Idaho Potato Commission, Idaho State Historical Society, Independence National Historical Park/C.W. Peale, iStock Photo, Library of Congress, Mile High Maps, Mountain High Maps, National Park Service, North Wind Picture Archives, One Mile Up, and Peter Arnold Inc., PhotoResearchers, U.S. Army, and the University of Idaho.
Statistics: State population statistics taken from 2008 U.S. Census Bureau estimates. City and town population statistics taken from July 1, 2007, U.S. Census Bureau estimates. Land and water area statistics taken from 2000 Census, U.S. Census Bureau.

Manufactured with paper containing at least 10% post-consumer waste

Library of Congress Cataloging-in-Publication Data

Ollhoff, Jim, 1959-
  Idaho / Jim Ollhoff.
     p. cm. -- (The United States)
  Includes index.
  ISBN 978-1-60453-647-8
  1. Idaho--Juvenile literature. I. Title.

F746.3.O45 2009
979.6--dc22

                              2008051038

Table of Contents

The Gem State 4

Quick Facts 6

Geography 8

Climate and Weather 12

Plants and Animals 14

History 18

Did You Know? 24

People 26

Cities 30

Transportation 34

Natural Resources 36

Industry 38

Sports 40

Entertainment 42

Timeline 44

Glossary 46

Index 48

The Gem State

Idaho is a state with huge areas of wilderness. Large sections of Idaho are mountains and forests.

The exact beginning of the name "Idaho" is a mystery. It may have been a Native American word. Another possibility is that the *Idaho* was a steamship that took people toward Idaho's gold fields.

In the 1860s, a candidate for Congress told people that Idaho was a Native American word that meant "gem of the mountains." Even though this probably wasn't true, the name stuck. Idaho has been called "The Gem State" ever since.

Today, Idaho has many industries. Perhaps most famous is the Idaho potato. More potatoes are grown in Idaho than any other state.

Idaho is a state with huge areas of unspoiled wilderness.

Quick Facts

Name: Uncertain. Idaho was probably named after a steamship that regularly traveled up the Columbia River.

State Capital: Boise

Date of Statehood: July 3, 1890 (43rd state)

Population: 1,523,816 (39th-most populous state)

Area (Total Land and Water): 83,570 square miles (216,445 sq km), 14th-largest state

Largest City: Boise, population 202,832

Nickname: The Gem State

Motto: *Esto Perpetua* (Let it be forever)

State Bird: Mountain Bluebird

State Flower: Syringa

State Gem: Idaho Star Garnet

State Tree: Western White Pine

State Song: "Here We Have Idaho"

Highest Point: Borah Peak, 12,662 feet (3,859 m)

Lowest Point: Snake River, 710 feet (216 m)

Average July Temperature: 87°F (31°C)

Record High Temperature: 118°F (48°C) at Orofino, July 28, 1934

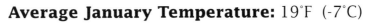

Average January Temperature: 19°F (-7°C)

Record Low Temperature: -60°F (-51°C) at Island Park Dam, January 18, 1943

Borah Peak

Average Annual Precipitation: 19 inches (48 cm)

Number of U.S. Senators: 2

Number of U.S. Representatives: 2

Snake River

U.S. Postal Service Abbreviation: ID

Geography

Much of Idaho is still wilderness. The state has more than 2.5 million acres (over 1 million hectares) of untouched beauty. Mountains, lakes, rivers, and gorges make up the beautiful scenery.

The far north part of Idaho is called the panhandle. It is only about 45 miles (72 km) wide. The southern part of the state is 310 miles (499 km) wide east to west.

The Snake River winds its way across the bottom of the state. This mighty river and its offshoots provide hydroelectric power for many people. The Snake River also provides irrigation to farmers' fields. Most of Idaho's population lives in cities and towns along the Snake River.

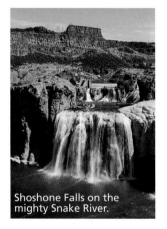
Shoshone Falls on the mighty Snake River.

Idaho's total land and water area is 83,570 square miles (216,445 sq km). It is the 14th-largest state. The state capital is Boise.

In the central and northern parts of the state there are huge forests and mountains. The Sawtooth Range and the Salmon River Mountains are found here. The highest point in Idaho is Borah Peak in the Lost River Mountain Range. One of the deepest gorges in North America is Hells Canyon, which goes as low as 7,900 feet (2,408 m) below the neighboring mountains.

Hells Canyon is one of the deepest river gorges in North America. The Snake River winds through it. The Seven Devils Mountain Range soars above. Many people enjoy the area's rugged beauty.

More than 2,000 lakes dot the Idaho map. Lake Pend Oreille and Priest Lake are large lakes with great fishing. Idaho residents boast that Lake Coeur d'Alene is the world's most beautiful lake.

Idaho borders six states. Washington and Oregon are to the west of Idaho. Montana and Wyoming are found to the east of the state. Nevada and Utah are at the south. The Canadian province of British Columbia is to the north of Idaho.

Idaho residents boast that Lake Coeur d'Alene is the world's most beautiful lake.

Climate and Weather

Even though Idaho does not border the Pacific Ocean, this ocean still influences the weather of the state. Wet air called "humidity" drifts in from the Pacific Ocean, especially in winter. This makes Idaho's winters warmer than other northern states.

Large parts of northern Idaho get an average of 40-50 inches (102-127 cm) of rain and snow each year. Much of southern Idaho averages less than 15 inches (38 cm) of precipitation per year. There is more snow in the mountains than in the plains.

In Boise, the largest city, January temperatures average 29 degrees Fahrenheit (–2°C). In July, Boise temperatures average 74 degrees Fahrenheit (23°C).

Tornadoes are rare, but do occur in Idaho. The state does see severe storms, sometimes with strong winds and hail.

A lightning storm over Boise, Idaho.

Plants and Animals

Nearly 40 percent of Idaho is forest, mostly in the northern mountainous areas. White and western fir, white pine, and Douglas fir are common trees in the forests. Aspen, maple, willow, mountain ash, and birch are also found in areas surrounding the mountains.

In the southern forests, ponderosa pine, lodgepole pine, and Douglas fir grow to great heights.

The mountains and forests of Idaho have few people and only scattered roads. Since animals like to be away from people, these remote areas are home to many different creatures. Idaho is one of the few states where grizzly bears, mountain lions, and wolves still roam. Rocky Mountain goats, elk, big horn sheep, mule deer, and many smaller animals are also common.

A mountain lion chases a hare.

Gray Wolf

Bighorn Sheep

Elk

A migrating chinook salmon leaps its way through white water in Idaho's Rapid River.

Largemouth and smallmouth bass are found in lakes and rivers throughout Idaho. Crappie, bluegill, walleye, and perch also are common. Steelhead rainbow trout and salmon spend many months in the ocean, and then return to Idaho to spawn.

Sturgeon can be found in the Snake, Kootenai, and Salmon Rivers. Sturgeon are huge fish. The largest on record weighed 394 pounds (179 kg).

Today there are fewer and fewer sturgeon. Fish hatcheries and farms help keep sturgeon from becoming extinct.

History

A Nez Percé warrior chief.

People have lived in the Idaho area for 10,000 to 15,000 years. By the 1700s, several Native American tribes called this region home. The Nez Percé lived in the northern part of Idaho, along with the Kutenai and Salish. Northern Paiutes lived in the west side of the state. Western Shoshone and the Northern Shoshone tribes lived in the southern areas of the region.

Probably the first Europeans in the area were members of the Lewis and Clark Expedition in 1805. Meriwether Lewis and William Clark explored the land on their way to the Pacific Ocean. Not long afterwards, trappers and hunters arrived in the rich land that would later become Idaho.

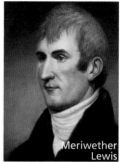

Meriwether Lewis

William Clark

The Lemhi Pass, on the Idaho and Montana border, looks much the same today as when Meriwether Lewis and William Clark traveled over it in 1805.

In 1809, a trading post was set up on Lake Pend Oreille, in the northern part of the state. This was the first settlement by white settlers. Trappers and missionaries soon moved in.

By the 1840s, wagon trains traveled through the area on their way to California.

The state's population boomed in 1860 with the discovery of gold on the Clearwater River. Gold was discovered in other places in the years that followed.

Idaho's Dewey Gold Mine operated from Thunder Mountain in 1903.

Potatoes are bagged during a harvest in Twin Falls, Idaho.

In 1863, Idaho Territory was formed. More settlers arrived. Farmers began planting potatoes. To this day, Idaho is famous for its potatoes.

Native Americans tried to stop the loss of their land. The United States Army and the Native American tribes fought battles in the 1850s, 1860s, and 1870s. Eventually, all the local tribes were forced to move to reservations.

University of Idaho's original Administration Building in 1900.

Other events in the late 1800s populated the state. Railroads were completed, creating economic growth. Lead and silver were mined. Sheep and cattle ranches were started in the area. In 1889, the University of Idaho was established.

A power plant on the Snake River in 1911.

Early in the 1900s, the federal government helped in the development of hydroelectric plants. These plants use river water to make electricity. Lumber became an important industry in the early 1900s.

During World War I (1914-1918), the war effort needed the food grown by Idaho farmers. This brought good economic times to the state. But as the war ended and the Great Depression hit, Idaho residents suffered.

World War II (1939-1945) again helped Idaho's economy. The country needed Idaho's farm products, as well as metals from the state's mines.

During World War II, the country was filled with fear. Some people thought that Japanese Americans might try to help Japan and hurt America. The U.S. government arrested

The Minidoka Relocation Center housed thousands of Japanese Americans during World War II.

many Japanese Americans. More than 10,000 of these citizens were shipped to relocation camps in Idaho.

Idaho grew in the 1970s. However, drought and grasshopper swarms hurt agriculture in the mid-1980s.

Today, Idaho has an economy of many different parts. Agriculture, manufacturing, and tourism are important to the state's economy.

Did You Know?

Chief Joseph (1840?–1904) was a smart and respected leader of the Nez Percé tribe. The Nez Percé were a powerful tribe, and usually friendly to the incoming white settlers. However, the U.S. government continued to take away their lands, and forced the Nez Percé onto small reservations.

In 1877, after a few Nez Percé warriors killed a number of white settlers, Chief Joseph feared that the U.S. Army would seek revenge. He quickly gathered his people, and led them on a 1,000-mile (1,600 km) journey toward Canada. The U.S. Army lost several battles chasing Chief Joseph and his people across Idaho and Montana.

Chief Joseph won the respect of many by his concern for women and children, as well as his honesty. Rather than stealing, he purchased supplies for his tribe's trip.

After a three-month chase, the U.S. Army finally caught Chief Joseph

Chief Joseph surrenders to General Nelson Miles.

and his people. Only 40 miles (64 km) from Canada, he surrendered. His speech became famous: "Hear me, my chiefs; my heart is sick and sad. From where the sun now stands, I will fight no more forever."

In 1879, he visited President Rutherford Hayes. In 1903, he traveled to see President Theodore Roosevelt. Both times Chief Joseph tried to help his people. But he was never allowed to return to his homeland. He died in 1904.

People

Sculptor **Gutzon Borglum** (1867–1941) was born in St. Charles, Idaho. He and his parents moved to Nebraska when he was young. He studied art. He became interested in large sculptures. He first carved a giant

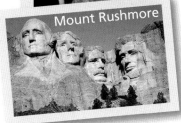

Mount Rushmore

head of Abraham Lincoln in a six-ton (5.4-metric-ton) block of marble. In 1927, South Dakota asked him to carve the heads of four great presidents into the side of Mount Rushmore. George Washington's likeness was completed in 1930. Thomas Jefferson was completed in 1936, Abraham Lincoln in 1937. Theodore Roosevelt's likeness was finished in 1939. Borglum died in 1941, leaving his son, Lincoln, to complete the final details.

Harmon Killebrew (1936–) was a baseball player for the Minnesota Twins. He was born in Payette, Idaho. He played high school sports there. Baseball scouts saw him play the game in 1954, and signed him. His raw strength enabled him to hit many home runs. Local fans called him Harmon "kill a few" because of his long home run hits. He retired in 1975, after hitting 573 home runs. In 1984, he was inducted into the Baseball Hall of Fame.

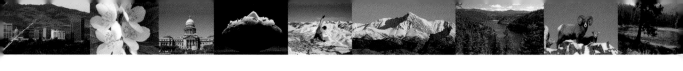

Author **Edgar Rice Burroughs** (1875–1950) was born in Chicago, Illinois, but spent many of his early years in Idaho. He worked odd jobs before writing his first novel. In 1912, he wrote his first story about Tarzan, a boy raised by apes in the jungles of Africa. He wrote 25 books about Tarzan, all of which were very popular. The stories were translated into 56 languages. Some were made into comic books, television shows, and movies. He wrote a large number of other novels, most of them science fiction. During World War II, he became a war reporter.

Walt Disney Pictures' 1999 animated *Tarzan*.

Picabo Street

(1971–) was born in the tiny town of Triumph, Idaho. Her first name is pronounced "peek-a-boo," and is a Sho-Ban Indian  word for "shining waters." In the 1990s, she was one of the best downhill skiers in the world. At age six, she was already skiing at Sun Valley Ski Resort near her home. By the age of 17, she made the U.S. Ski Team. During the 1994 Olympic Winter Games, she won a silver medal. Despite a serious knee injury, she won a gold medal in the 1998 Olympic Winter Games. She retired after the 2002 Olympics with many medals, honors, and championships to her name.

Cities

Boise is the largest city in Idaho, with a population of 202,832. The neighboring towns and suburbs bring the population to over 600,000. Boise is the state capital. French pioneers probably named the city in the 1820s. These mountain men named the nearby river "La Riviere Boise," meaning, "the wooded river." In the 1830s, Fort Boise was founded. Boise has a wide variety of service and manufacturing industries. It is the home of Boise State University. Also, the city has campuses of Idaho State University, the University of Idaho, and George Fox University.

Idaho Falls was originally the site of a bridge over the Snake River. In 1865, businessman Matt Taylor built the bridge. It became known as Taylor's Crossing. The bridge helped travelers, new settlers, and the U.S.

Taylor's Crossing

Army. With so many people arriving at the crossing, a town sprang up. The town was named Eagle Rock. In 1891, town leaders changed the name to Idaho Falls. Today Idaho Falls is a center for health care in the area. Many small businesses, restaurants, and computer firms round out the city's economy. Eastern Idaho Technical College is one of the colleges in the city. The population of Idaho Falls is 53,279.

Pocatello is one of the bigger cities in Idaho, with a population of 54,572. In 1834, a fur trader set up a trading post a little north of where the city is today.

The post became an important stop on the Oregon Trail. Gold was discovered in the area in 1860. Many settlers and treasure hunters came to the area at that time. Railroads came through in the late 1870s, again increasing the city's importance. The city is named after Native American Chief Pocatello of the Shoshone tribe.

Pocatello, Idaho, in 1909.

Coeur d'Alene was founded in 1878 as a trading post. The founders named the city after the Native American tribe that lived in the area. The city grew when lead and silver were discovered in 1883. It grew even more when the railroads arrived in 1886. Today, Coeur d'Alene has a population of 42,267. Lumbering is a big industry in the city. Coeur d'Alene is also a popular tourist destination. The city is home to North Idaho College. The University of Idaho and the Lewis-Clark State College also have campuses there.

Transportation

Interstate 90 goes east and west on the north side of the state. Interstates 86 and 84 go east and west in the south side of the state. Interstate 15 goes north and south through eastern Idaho.

Idaho's mountains and wilderness can make travel difficult at times.

Idaho's mountains and wilderness sometimes make travel difficult. To get around the state, transportation by airplane is important. There are six commercial airports in Idaho. Boise Airport is the largest airport in the state.

A plane helps firefighters control a fire near Viola, Idaho.

There are more than 100 airports, airfields, and airstrips in Idaho, and many private fliers. The United States Forest Service uses these airfields in their work.

The Burlington Northern Santa Fe Railway runs across the northern part of the state. The Union Pacific Railroad crosses southern Idaho.

Natural Resources

Gold was discovered in the 1800s, and that brought many settlers to Idaho. However, gold mining is no longer important to the state's economy. Today, Idaho's mines produce silver, lead, and other metals. Phosphate mining and processing is also a big industry.

Lucky Friday Mine in Silver Valley.

About 22 million acres (9 million ha) of Idaho are rangeland. This is land where nothing is built. Grasses and vegetation grow. About 20 million acres (8 million ha) are forestland. Nearly 8 million acres (3 million ha) of land is used for agriculture.

Although known for its potatoes, Idaho also has many wheat farms.

Agriculture is important to Idaho. The state is the number one producer of potatoes in the United States. In fact, about one-third of all the potatoes eaten in the United States are from Idaho. Wheat is another large crop, along with Austrian winter peas.

There are almost 25,000 farms in Idaho. Dairy cattle produce 7 million pounds (3 million kg) of milk each year. The state's chickens lay more than 249 million eggs per year.

Industry

In the early 1800s, the area's first industry was trapping. Mountain men found many animals with beautiful furs. By the 1860s, mining became important. Then, agriculture became

A cowboy herds cattle on an Idaho ranch.

the most important industry. Beef cattle, sheep, wheat, barley, and the famous Idaho potato are all part of the state's agriculture. In the 1900s, the timber industry also grew the state's economy.

Today, agriculture, mining, food processing, timber, and manufacturing are the biggest industries in Idaho. Science and high-tech manufacturing has grown.

A snowboarder in action above popular Sun Valley, Idaho.

Another fast-growing industry is tourism. Idaho's unspoiled wilderness and large recreational areas attract many people to the state. Central Idaho's Sun Valley is one of the most famous vacation spots in the United States.

Sports

Idaho has no major league sports teams, but there are minor league teams. Minor leagues prepare players to be on professional teams. The Boise Hawks and the Idaho Falls Chukars are minor league baseball teams. The Idaho Steelheads are a minor league ice hockey team that plays in Boise. The Idaho Stampede plays minor league basketball in Boise.

Because of Idaho's great wilderness area, big game hunting is popular. Moose, pronghorn, bighorn sheep, and even bear and mountain lions are hunted.

Idaho manages hunting very carefully so that animal populations don't get too small or too large.

National forests, national trails, and numerous state parks provide plenty of opportunity for camping, hiking, and nature watching. Idaho has great ski resorts and plenty of other outdoor recreation.

Rafting is a popular sport on Idaho's many rivers.

Entertainment

Idaho has many historical museums. The largest is the Idaho Historical Museum in Boise. Its many artifacts and education programs tell of the state's history, from dinosaur times to the present.

A number of the larger cities have orchestras. Idaho's universities have choirs, symphonies, and theaters.

There are many fairs and festivals. The North Idaho

A snow and ice sculpture created during the McCall Winter Carnival.

Fair & Rodeo is a popular summer event for the north side of the state. January in McCall, Idaho, brings the week-long McCall Winter Carnival.

There is an annual bluegrass music festival in Pocatello. There is even a gathering where people can hear cowboy poetry.

A popular music event is the Lionel Hampton International Jazz Festival at the University of Idaho in Moscow, on the northwest side of the state. Since 1967, great jazz musicians have come together with young and old jazz students to celebrate their music.

Jazzman Lionel Hampton

Jazzman Hank Jones

Jazz pianist Hank Jones signs autographs for young jazz fans during the Lionel Hampton International Jazz Festival in Moscow, Idaho.

Timeline

1700s—Several Native American tribes call this region home. These tribes include the Nez Percé, Kutenai, Salish, Northern Paiutes, and Shoshone.

1805—Meriwether Lewis and William Clark, with their expedition, explore the area.

1809—A trading post is set up on Pend Oreille Lake.

1840s—Wagon trains travel through Idaho on their way to California.

1860—Gold is discovered on the Clearwater River.

1863—Idaho Territory is formed.

1874—The first railroad is established at Franklin, Idaho.

1890—Idaho becomes the 43rd state.

Early 1900s—Hydroelectric power plants are developed.

1906—The country's largest sawmill opens in Potlatch, Idaho.

1936—The Sun Valley resort opens. They feature the country's first ski lift.

1939-1945—World War II helps Idaho economically.

1984—Idaho native Harmon Killebrew is elected to the Baseball Hall of Fame.

Glossary

Great Depression—A time in American history beginning in 1929 and lasting for several years when many businesses failed across the country and millions of people lost their jobs.

Hydroelectric—A way of generating electricity that uses water rather than burning oil or coal.

Kutenai—A Native American tribe living in Idaho, Washington state, and British Columbia, Canada, before the arrival of the Europeans.

Lewis and Clark Expedition—An expedition led by Meriwether Lewis and William Clark, who explored the north and west parts of the United States from 1804 to 1806.

Nez Percé—A Native American tribe living in Idaho before the arrival of the Europeans. Chief Joseph was the leader of the Nez Percé in the late 1800s to early 1900s.

Paiutes—A Native American tribe living in Idaho before the arrival of the Europeans.

Panhandle—The narrow strip of land that is the north side of the state.

Salish—A Native American tribe living in Idaho before the arrival of the Europeans.

Shoshone—A Native American tribe living in Idaho before the arrival of the Europeans.

Wilderness—An area that has retained its natural beauty, untouched by human hands.

World War I— A war that was fought in Europe from 1914 to 1918, involving countries around the world. The United States entered the war in April 1917.

World War II—A conflict across the world, lasting from 1939-1945. The United States entered the war in December 1941.

Index

A
Africa 28
America 23
Army, U.S. 21, 24, 25, 31

B
Baseball Hall of Fame 27
Boise, ID 12, 30, 40
Boise Airport 34
Boise Hawks 40
Boise State University 30
Borah Peak 10
Borglum, Gutzon 26
Borglum, Lincoln 26
British Columbia, Canada 11
Burlington Northern Santa Fe Railway 35
Burroughs, Edgar Rice 28

C
California 20
Canada 24, 25
Chicago, IL 28
Clark, William 18
Clearwater River 20
Coeur d'Alene, ID 33
Coeur d'Alene, Lake 11
Congress 4

E
Eagle Rock, ID 31
Eastern Idaho Technical College 31

F
Fort Boise 30

G
George Fox University 30
Great Depression 22

H
Hayes, Rutherford 25
Hells Canyon 10

I
Idaho (steamship) 4
Idaho Falls, ID 31
Idaho Falls Chukars 40
Idaho Historical Museum 42
Idaho Stampede 40
Idaho State University 30
Idaho Steelheads 40
Idaho Territory 21

J
Japan 23
Jefferson, Thomas 26
Joseph, Chief 24, 25

K
Killebrew, Harmon 27
Kootenai River 17
Kutenai (tribe) 18

L
La Riviere Boise 30
Lewis, Meriwether 18
Lewis-Clark State College 33
Lincoln, Abraham 26
Lionel Hampton International Jazz Festival 43
Lost River Mountain Range 10

M
McCall, ID 42
McCall Winter Carnival 42
Minnesota Twins 27
Montana 11
Moscow, ID 43

N
Nebraska 26
Nevada 11
Nez Percé (tribe) 18, 24
North America 10
North Idaho College 33
Northern Idaho Fair & Rodeo 42

O
Olympics 29
Oregon 11
Oregon Trail 32

P
Pacific Ocean 12, 18
Paiute (tribe) 18
Payette, ID 27
Pend Oreille, Lake 11, 20
Pocatello, Chief 32
Pocatello, ID 32, 43
Priest Lake 11

R
Roosevelt, Theodore 25, 26
Rushmore, Mount 26

S
Salish (tribe) 18
Salmon River 17
Salmon River Mountains 10
Sawtooth Range 10
Sho-Ban (tribe) 29
Shoshone (tribe) 18, 32
Snake River 8, 17, 31
South Dakota 26
St. Charles, ID 26
Street, Picabo 29
Sun Valley, ID 39
Sun Valley Ski Resort 29

T
Tarzan 28
Taylor, Matt 31
Taylor's Crossing 31
Triumph, ID 29

U
Union Pacific Railroad 35
United States 37, 39
United States Forest Service 35
United States Ski Team 29
University of Idaho 22, 30, 33, 43
Utah 11

W
Washington 11
Washington, George 26
World War I 22
World War II 23, 28
Wyoming 11